of port & hues

# of port & hues

by

dylan rice-leary

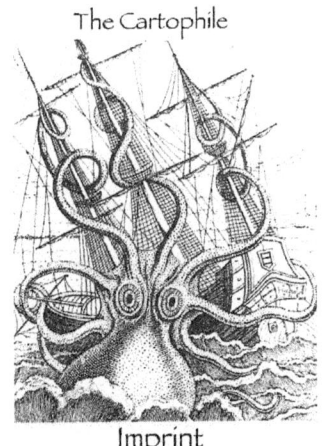

for Ella   ~   123%

of port & hues – by dylan rice-leary

ISBN 978-0-557-82230-0

All poems written in 2010 at 260 N. Padre Juan Ave – Meiners Oaks, CA.

Copyright © 2010 by dylan rice-leary.
A Cartophile Imprint, Portland, OR.
http://thecartophileimprint.com
All rights reserved.
No part of this book may be reproduced in any form or by any electronic or mechanical means including information storage and retrieval systems, without permission in writing from the author.
The only exception is by a reviewer, who may quote short excerpts.

Cover & back-cover photographs by dylan rice-leary.

contents:

falling rise, spring of fall-	1
made did an unmaking do	2
the void	3
i am a hyphen	4
in remembrance of remembrance	5
in the nightsuit stiched	6
cumquat/loquat	7
the taste is next to nothing	8
to out sea horizon	9
is it past a thought	10
it is for them we live to turn our phases of the moon	11
if eyes wider &	12
here: at the chub lip	13
in stance askance	14
ode to a mazzy star cd	15
by gosh & golly, mercuroids	16
for martyred offerings	17
i was walking & it's morning &	19
even so	21
tendrils to the trellis	22

w/ omen   23

in testament   24

twelve to one   25

to the mothers   26

life is beach   27

my bark is worse   28

night vision   29

lady bootleather/downfeather   30

(of which there are many)   31

am candelabra   32

by stork   33

my uncommon wordling   34

ope, fledge - for   35

dr. peptic   36

mollusks we   37

under the mask   38

w/ hackles & vigor   39

solemn eerily   40

spf godblock   41

we brachiate   42

eros of erosion   43

sweet is the just bit	44
fists of root	45
why don't we do it in the past	46
unkosher nights	47
discriminate w/ idyll	48
insect of the los angeles basin	49
when hope decrees ordinance	50
unplastered alice	51
thrum of blood	52
not all swallows	54
vulcan dog-collar	55
infantity	56
of pylons &	57
what do you do when it rains?	58

of

port

&

hues

d y l a n   r i c e − l e a r y

falling rise, the spring of fall-

falling rise, the spring of fall-
the fruit it ripes to picking's pluck
& all autumnal harvest hands
uplift to greet you in your seasons.

& in the turning of the leaf &
fore the void of winter's chill,
we fill our barrels, jams to can-
bounties in our sunken pantries,
meat is salted in its larder
& all that's jerked and jellied is for keeping.

& in our sundry stores - all goods as these
are suched for morrow's making,
a laying on all tables
to feast our dark nights thru.

made did an unmaking do

what is done is done

&

what is made is made,

but what's been made can be undone

& undone makings make anew.

& in the doings not undone i've did

& do again, i'll do-

& in the making of undoing i'm

unmade by this making done.

(& in the whitelight of evening

& darkness of our morns, all may

dare to gaze upon the sun & stare.)

& making done & doing made

& made the did to do again

(and again,)

again, i'll do.

the void

the void

at heart

is empty-

no matter

what

it says.

i am a hyphen

a bridge. a stile.

the in-between of things.

i am connect & born to twain.

i am unspoken "and" & of ampersand.

w/o time's devoid of space,

& phrase-as-concept's hard on eyes.

i am nothing but a dash,

a line,

i am the broken word rejoined.

i prelude to the suffix-which-stands-alone.

i am the gift of undecided nomenclature.

i am an awkward sign of equal stance-

of father and of mother both,

or mother and of father.

the primacy of sequence rests on all of you who use me.

in remembrance of remembrance

in remembrance of remembrance
i will raise yesteryear's glasses,
& shed a single kindergarten tear
for each fallen leaf in all my autumns.

& i will forever look forward to
one thousand last-friday nights
& each and every weekend breakfast had.

& i cannot wait to see all those i've seen
& those i will not see again
& eagerly expect each sound already heard.

i am waiting for each brush of skin
i've ever touched-
& i'm anticipating one and all that has transpired.

& unto all that's been, i will raise yesteryear's glasses.

in the nightsuit stitched

in the darkness we can
see to never touch
again the sun,
& yet it always
comes to always come.

in the nightsuit stitched
& thimble-threaded unto blood,
we can seem to never get the skin
& yet it always comes
to come when cloth undone.

in the godhead we who
seek to speak
but not today in tongues,
always it comes to us again
in whispered drum.

& in the artless wail

of brokenhearts

& deeds ill-done,

there is a sun,

there is a skin,

there is a drum,

that's yet to come.

cumquat / loquat

"ah, cumquat" sd i & the eye
that eye gave her sd, "whoa,
loquat - you feed me."

eattheskin & spit
wet pits into my hand.

the taste is next to nothing

the taste is next to nothing
you've yet held on tongue,

we made out on helium.

to register for the exchange
brandished w/ receipt-

thesun&sky take all kinds of balloons.

to out sea horizon

to out sea horizon,

sharp coins & win

-ds in blindglint eyes~

reknow the form respiring-

the cresting swell,

the jetty cut,

the spume of reef

& scabbing foam-

(where love's from

there:

the holding coast,

themother&theson,

& the salty gull

all wavering & (in) particular.

is it past a thought

is it past a thought
to spend pennysense
on grimy dimes?

germing of the $,
waitress daughter
dirty hands back change
from sullied register:

a village gesture-
infect reciprocal
w/ contagions and gratuity;
in such sick we
enact our modern commerce.

it is for them we live to turn our phases of the moon

      wax stentorian, senator-

      for all the orators portend

      a newmoons simply spoke

      (nee hub

      in ray of lunar cyclings.

      yet you & i know both

      limber werewolves & night

      mother witches (dancing tween

      the shadow & the sea,

      that spell in intricate

      grammars.

so sit back down to earth, figurehead-
it is for them we live to turn our phases of the moon.

if eyes wider &

    if eyes wider &
        we'd see from i.r. to u.v.-
how i'd view you to me
for what stains & what thermal
would fail to zipper lips to private counsel?

  & will the shark
           - when yr in twopiece
electricmuzzle you more beautiful
    than i & does the honeybuzz bee detect
      a nectar
sweeter than ambrosial wetting-petal?
& what how just does spot nose
          upon these hands?
i understand that birdscan
foretell
            catastrophic
    happenings.
      i wonder what they'd wing
    of
storms as these.

    phenomena has girth, my octopus

(& lateral horizons
    so look me in the compound-
  i
& forever to me talk senses.

here: at the chub lip

here: at the chub lip

of consequence -

brimming on the tongue,

an uttered plosive from

butjust & stedded.

so: parceled in our shipping,

our mercantile waverings

portend a vasseling

to endless swayings of

all tidings~

hence: wet a finger

to the wind & raise

your white sails!

for guided by stars,

a far off port

is just a door

a(ny)way.

in stance askance

in stance askance
undained in watchful i's,
a pluraled palsy hush
es over ers of onlook.
& as the twins entwined
to staff bewing-
ed & serpented a
caduceus do,
so healing comes from
forked tongues
& licks us in the doing.

ode to a mazzy star cd

standoverus, hope sandoval!

& lo yr melencholera

on somber tollings

hithertoo unnaked

in the aster.

moan the lonesome sailor

home at last

from distant nazareth

& nuzzled in yr mutle-throated

offerings to pantheons-

all is mauve & groovy.

by gosh & golly, mercuroids-

by gosh & golly, mercuroids-
your pull is full & pluraled:
the swifting wit a catalyst
for benders in the archives~

bookending twin (begun again
& wet a finger to the page
shall turn for all the words
in all the verses
of all worlds -

(for as i & i make ii -
our straightening of anything
just so a chance to bend
between the poles we pluck the
lines & thrum the many from the few,
so the many faces in the facets
of the gem. & i w/o ii
doesn't do.

for martyred offerings

lark darts hitheree & to
thru sunlipped yards &
airspace indefinite
to the chagrin of fallen seeds
everywhere- for we are beyond
well zoned in this & more.

to wing bygone periphery
in lights of spring &
nary a hawking eye under
which to tremble
on this low noon-

the cooing dove,
the beating thrush,
(atwitter by the caw
of local murders & the
vimming of the jay - all
sing of that which
wiggles neath the earth.

as such the grub

& so the worm

& ergo even mole-

all liminal in june.

for these unlikely magi

three blindwisemen

bear no myrrh,

& fixed on stars

for martyred offerings

subsumed as gift to birth.

i was walking & it's morning &

i was walking & it's morning &
i wander are you all around in
picket-fence soft places
wholly cul de sacrament
taken in planned community.

& hallowed are your gray still temples open
to all vagabonds & transience
in streetlamp light of tracts as these.

& does he honey-home you
in all the living room you've
borne to mortgage. what the
cost & who the deed &
how are you on storage?
& does he palm the purchased
egg & does he grind
your beans. & when he
makesitforyouinbed - have you truly

broken fast?

i

was just wandering

since

i was walking &

it's morning.

even so

even so there is no quibble
over meaning what we say
to mean to one another -
things must be even so

you go first & i will
wait since that's what we're
so good at afterall

even so there is no way
to one another
under meaning what we mean
to say we say

even so there must be
even so.

tendrils to the trellis

train yr tendrils to the trellis,

morningglory - all over yrself

(fingers in nooks - runners laying cop to crook

in climbing

walls & clinging at the wire~

& mid the purplethick petal lip&bulbing-

reaching gloriana greets the daylord

(hello, sunshine.

w/omen

windchimes knell to the sixth house of loneliness

& rising signs signify justabit too much

in our ponderous porchorbit.

when mercury's in renegade & venus,

conjunct & sextile, ouijaes

feathers - mind the skies.

not all w/omen come shaped like birds

but some do

(butsomedo

in testament

to talk w/ you's confession
(& of prayer)

to speak of is a catechism-
& genuflected
to yr mass i am sermoned.

& in you i take communion
(the body & the blood
upon my psalms,
i cross myself to the book.
& on my knees in hymn to you-

i am reborn, lover.

twelve to one

you are&i believe

it teaming & pull the sun.

(as i swim

you are the ram & i- porpoise,

a schooling of neptuna.

i believe&you are

eponymously striking me

(day-thru ~ night-thru)

for we are softly steaming.

& to yr hoofing blaze & arcing skyward pathings

i will hold you in the seas when you comet

to my oceans - or splash-

down in these harbors, i

always - mission of apollo,

will catch you on night's reentry.

you&i are believe
it born of depth & fire,
for midst our rose-red fingers,
tomorrow you will rise from me again~

twelve to one.

to the mothers

to the mothers i have met
along the way from then til now,

i would like to make you dinner.

life is beach

in tidepools south of the estuary,

silt deposits give to what juts-

&-cups in rough cradles

of anemone-flowers & mussel-beds.

shoaled - wetfoot & undersun,

(w/ crustacea & conch to the kelp,

we are humble in the wash~

treading careful.

& in wading for what may not be already found,

life abounds.

my bark is worse

apocalypse of mentholated diarrhea-
eucalyptus spring-eternal
pissing seed & cone
& hotshit spicey leaf,

control yr bladder!
oh, you mighty incontinent & besotted arbor~

who do you think you are?

(& although i piss on yr leg,
please don't go on my lawn.

night vision

late visitor ~ o' haunter
of the house of me
(tho you are welcome & i invite you in
so vivid you are almost real.

mad-laughter & low-moanings
echo in this vaulted room.
& you just shake those chains you wear
when all i want, ghostling, is to hold you.

(unlocked:
the key is to not be scared
& to forget that you are not here
in body as you are in spirit.

but i beg you - be careful, specter ~
for i know where your bones lay
& for them to hold against my own,
i am both above & not.

lady bootleather/downfeather

lady bootleather, sit awhile
on whiteleather couched evenings
in this spring of our summer.

lady downfeather, lay away
by lamplight nested & wet-feathered
in these eyes of our hearts.

(of which there are many)

by skinflush heatrush i
ope pheremonad to the verse
(of which there are many)

by hotgush bloodblush you
soup to be the trothe
(of which there are also many)

by lovelush lighttouch we
scattertale on multitudes
& rise up to the one
(of which there are more than many)

& from suchbrush we cull the cutting
& plant into a single earth.

am candelabra

well - sconced to   pallor ~ inflammable
(in shadow) enshelved,
we sit
above wainscot
& vantaged on mantle
(in shadow)   (am candelabra)

by stork-

by stork-

mortaled maculate

& albatrossed

to these aerial planes,

so :

w/ such terrible touching

-downs,

that suffering is runway

oft aborted.

my uncommon wordling

my uncommon wordling,
   you hot yiddish slang-

(just to speak on the lips)

& w/ plosives & sibilance~
   in you i am fluent.

ope, fledge – for

ope, fledge - for
you are over down, now
proud-feathered tail & pin.

perched nestly:
& from there to ground

is a lifetime.

dr. peptic

foreign antibody reject
adverse interior.
(hicc-
brightlight white-cell entreaty
sposed antidoting on
what is prolly curative.
-up)
& utterly proachable
mannered bedside.

mollusks we

eight arms am eye
complex us in focus,
mutable
~cranny, hue & span.

flux mussel flex-jet~
symmetric
the pearl is your oyster,
& we swim in oceans.

under the mask

poulticed in adam's clay,

a porous slab-offering -

always~sutured umbilical & rib

(& eve is the rib

& abel the scab

as cain the scar

(& eve is forever the rib

& chesting heart,

we bear this mud to face it.

w/ hackles & vigor

bristled goose pimps

arise in pluraled infantries:

"over the top, boys- for god

& sweetsacred country."

& this is how able

men-in-arms die young~

w/ hackles &

vigor brimming.

solemn eerily

in lumens elongate
midst winds uneasy &
fronds in high places-
dislodge yard scarred in fists of palm

as mad dove coos relentless
& solemn eerily lit's
this late in day.

spf godblock

acolytes of the sun once

chosen ones of Ra

now daughters of topical cancerous lesions

what have you done

to save your skin

we brachiate

    cocksure and fancy

                      free we swing arboreal

  & boughing.   we brachiate-

              -to no place

        & everywhere

    in particular   jungles~

(when canopy   is second sky

        (where we are closer

            (to our gods

                (in heavens

eros of erosion

by mortar & pestle

we gristle to the grindstone -

& what it is   is   what it wasn't.

so the eros of erosion:

convex & concave

sweet is the just bit

when the fruit of consequence

hangs heavy on the vine,

pluck up your pluck, dear -

& shine to polish rubbed against your cotton.

for always sweet is the just bit,

& first-incisor tongues to molar

(as is natch.

heretofore an irish peach,

a palm of red delicious -

but never yet a ripened lubsk queen of porcelain skin,

harvested

& sequined on the chin.

fists of root

when the ghost
is in the guesthouse
& the visitor of excess
transes mirth to Bacchus~
the revelers who worship spirit
answer their own dark prayers

& not the demon rumble
nor a rebel cry of 'sic'
shall flap this chimney crow

when just as well
is just well pretended
& succulents uproot the stone-toad
& squirrels nibblegnaw upon the skull

-then is when the fists of root
rise clenched in common cause

why don't we do it in the past

why don't we do it

in the past?

no one will be

watching us why? don't

we do it in the pas-

-t

unkosher nights

stainhooved &
prescient i clopmark nocturnal
in hallways of dream

splain-foot~
i find my hunger open & w i d e
traversed to mind's eye

discriminate w/ idyll

sordid & suscpect to flora

land-scaper

reign raze designs

of stem & of node

cossack yr vinca major

denuding oak of iving vine

pan-violate

&

discriminate w/ idyll

hands of a butcher

insect of the los angeles basin

skim yellow waspling you
mulching dirt bride

striping the hunt
thorax & barb

yr parasitic-tock-
tic's beyond almanac

when hope decrees ordinance

braveproud deadman was

allglory epithet worth

widowed son

& has longended short-tooth

rebirthed the patriarch

when hope decrees

ordinance - even death

breaks voice

unplastered alice

unplastered alice licked
postage stamps

pasty-tonguedly
culling them to alba

thrum of blood

horses horses

always horses

& once again: decrepit

spirit-ghost

of Spider Web Forest

ravages me with prophetic visions

freakishly laughing

laughing

dreams of terrible power

& there you are with

blackened teeth &

ridiculous eye-brow horns

i am not vincible

you are not satiable

horses

horses

always horses

and running

Spider Web Castle
is ours; yet Spider
Web Forest is not
done with me

& you will see the seas incarnadine
& i will see murdered my best-friend

horses

& then i will be shot at
always am i shot at
by comically apocalyptic abundance
of choreographed arrow-volleys

and there is laughter from the forest
which frightens the
horses.

& do not let this sequence ever be forgot
for Spider Web Castle was real
& once truly stood where this is read

not all swallows

as the dusking sun
spits slender
shards upon the lawn,

we tender bird-
song into inkmark-

& pen-stroke to dog-bark
not all swallows
will see summer

vulcan dog-collar

metallurged & fitted i am
well-nigh trammeled by
silver grasp & measured gripping

-bound to at last-

infantity

infant transposes infinite

wide-eyed at the void

twixt a

cheek & jowl

hold fast & release

a thumb

with awful

-ly tiny hands

of pylons &

another detour road cone

road cone road

postings hued unmapping

valence & trajec

no turning left

oracular signage

in-direction & in-decision

of pylons &

shapes in-scribed

what do you do when it rains?

what do you do when it rains?
& what do you do when it storms?
do you differ in squall than to drizzle?
& what do you do when the sky cracks in two
& illuminates all for thunder and boom?

what do you do with a sprinkle?
what do you do with a drop?
& what do you do with the buckets,
the cats & the dogs, & where do you keep extra tarps?
and what do you do when it's raining?

do you think of rain dancing?
you think of mud streaking?
do you think of stoking the fire & of soup?
do you think of flames & of heat & of hearts
& yesteryear's weatherclouds over us breaking?

do you think like Noah and fear for the flood?
build boats - form arks - prepare for the pairing
& batten down hatches - a last bastioning
for God's will & yr own survival?

or do you think of Zeus when it thunders?
or remember what greek gods might lurk in the mists?
& will you recall the scorning of Hera
the next time the weather gives you wet kisses?

& what do you do in this element?
& how can any of us reciprocate such precipitate?

perhaps you will do as the rain does.
perhaps you will fall from above to the streets-
follow the path that resists you the least.
we might gather in gutters & puddle & pool-
somethings destroyed & others renewed.

do we splash in abandon & make mud not war?
do we dance on the roof - demand that we're heard?
do we sing you to sleep? do we keep you awake?
the patter & pound is of vector & rate.

do we give you ennui? does it give you the chills
for the aches in the bones - a payment for yesterday's bills
& purchases - no longer owned?
or does water-from-sky bring warmth to yr sweater?
& stomping in mud puddles make ya feel better?
is it the far of the fall? the drop of the drop?
when gathered in storm - how else could it stop?

for looking up often leads us to questions,
the whether of weather & wither to do,
ergo so in turn, i turn to the storm & ask:
what does rain do when it's you?

for what do you do in this element?
& how can any of us precipitates reciprocate suchly?

www.ingramcontent.com/pod-product-compliance
Lightning Source LLC
Chambersburg PA
CBHW061510040426
42450CB00008B/1543